Father and Son Journal

Fill In The Blank Prompted Journal To Get To Know Your Son Better

Catherine Adams

How to use this journal

Use the journal in the way that makes the most sense for you and your son. If he doesn't like to write, you can read and discuss the questions with him. If he enjoys writing, then you can take turns filling out the pages. If you need more space, there are blank pages in the back of the journal.

Use a thick piece of paper to hide your answers if you want to take turns. If there are questions that don't apply or that either of you don't like...skip them! Feel free to jump around or take turns picking questions; there is no specific order to them and no need to do every one.
I sincerely hope that you will be able to discuss your answers with each other, bond, and above all else, have fun!

My son and I are starting this journal

_____
(date)

My hope is that we will :

_____ have a little fun with it

_____ get to know each other a little better

_____ do a little bonding

_____ _____

If we complete at least _____ percent we will celebrate by:

_____

_____
(sign)

Son – answer

I have agreed to try this journal because:

_____   my dad asked me to

_____   I appreciate that he wants to
            get to know me better

_____   it was a gift

_____   _____

_____
(sign)

Your son woke up this morning with one of the following traits. Predict how he will rank his top 3. Rank your top three on the right.

Son		Dad
_____	Amazingly Athletic	_____
_____	Incredibly Handsome	_____
_____	Crazy Smart	_____
_____	Super Popular	_____
_____	Musically Gifted	_____

Optional: After you both have answered, discuss or write why you chose the traits you did or if you were surprised by each others choices:

_____

_____

_____

_____

_____

Son – answer

You woke up this morning with one of the following traits. Rank your top 3:

_____   Amazingly Athletic

_____   Incredibly Handsome

_____   Crazy Smart

_____   Super Popular

_____   Musically Gifted

Optional: After you both have answered, discuss or write why you chose the traits you did or if you were surprised by each others choices:

_____

_____

_____

_____

_____

CONGRATULATIONS...
You are now the
Supreme Ruler of Earth
and you may solve one World Problem
today........What will it be?

_____ Disease

_____ War/Terrorism

_____ Climate Change & Pollution

_____ Poverty/Starvation

_____ Drug/Substance Abuse

Why?_____

_____

_____

_____

_____

_____

CONGRATULATIONS...
You are now the
Supreme Ruler of Earth
and you may solve one World Problem
today........What will it be?

_____ Disease

_____ War/Terrorism

_____ Climate Change & Pollution

_____ Poverty/Starvation

_____ Drug/Substance Abuse

Why? _____

_____

_____

_____

_____

_____

When you were little where was the scariest place in your room?

_____ Under the bed

_____ In the closet

_____ Outside the window

_____ Somewhere else?

What did you think was hiding? What did you think would happen? (write/share/discuss)

_____

_____

_____

_____

_____

_____

_____

_____

_____

_____

Son – answer

When you were little where was the scariest place in your room?

_____   Under the bed

_____   In the closet

_____   Outside the window

_____   Somewhere else?

What did you think was hiding? What did you think would happen? (write/share/discuss)

_____

_____

_____

_____

_____

_____

_____

_____

_____

Dad – answer

What 2 things are you the most worried about regarding your son right now?

_____

_____

What 2 things are you the most worried about regarding your son in the future?

_____

_____

Optional: After you both have answered, discuss or write why you chose your answers or if you were surprised by each others choices:

_____
_____
_____
_____
_____
_____
_____

Son – answer

What 2 things are you the most worried about right now?

_____

_____

What 2 things are you the most worried about in the future?

_____

_____

Optional: After you both have answered, discuss or write why you chose your answers or if you were surprised by each others choices:

_____

_____

_____

_____

_____

_____

_____

About School....

This year what subject does your son...

do the best in?

_____

like the most?

_____

like the least?

_____

find the easiest?

_____

find the hardest?

_____

Optional: After you both have answered, discuss or write if you were surprised by each others choices:

_____

_____

_____

_____

_____

Son – answer second

About School....
This year what subject do you...

do the best in?

_____

like the most?

_____

like the least?

_____

find the easiest?

_____

find the hardest?

_____

Optional: After you both have answered, discuss or write if you were surprised by each others choices:

_____

_____

_____

_____

_____

Dad – can you draw ?

yourself

a cactus

a turtle

a ghost

Son - can you draw ?

yourself

a cactus

a turtle

a ghost

What are 2 ways you still treat your son like a little kid?

_____

_____

What are two ways you treat him like an adult?

_____

_____

Son – answer

Read what your dad wrote. Check the ones you agree with. If you want to add different things put them below:

_____

_____

_____

_____

CONGRATULATIONS...

You are now a member of one of the following...

Rank your preference and what you think your son will choose.

You   Son

_____   Seal Team 6   _____

_____   Knights of the
        Round Table   _____

_____   Ninjas   _____

_____   Vikings   _____

CONGRATULATIONS...

You are now a member of one of the following...

Rank your preference and what you think your dad will choose.

You   Dad

____ Seal Team 6   ____

____ Knights of the
      Round Table   ____

____ Ninjas   ____

____ Vikings   ____

Dad – answer

List 2 positive traits that would describe your son:

_____

_____

What is 1 thing he does that you appreciate?

What 2 positive traits would describe your dad?

_____

_____

What is 1 thing he does that you appreciate?

Dad – answer

Which of you .... more?

	Dad	Son
daydreams		
complains		
relaxes		
farts		
finds happiness in little things		
judges other people		
gives advice		
communicates		
has fun		

Son – answer

Which of you .... more?

	Dad	Son
daydreams		
complains		
relaxes		
farts		
finds happiness in little things		
judges other people		
gives advice		
communicates		
has fun		

List 2 fun things you think your son should do more of:

_____

_____

List 2 fun things you should do more of:

_____

_____

Write about a special memory of something you did together? (write/share/discuss)

_____

_____

_____

_____

_____

_____

_____

_____

_____

Son – answer

List 2 fun things you think your dad should do more of:

_____

_____

List 2 fun things you should do more of:

_____

_____

Write about a special memory of something you did together? (write/share/discuss)

_____

_____

_____

_____

_____

_____

_____

_____

YAY !!!
You just won a tattoo !!!
Are you happy or not?
(circle one)

What is it and where is it going?
(draw or write below)

YAY !!!
You just won a tattoo !!!
Are you happy or not?
(circle one)

What is it and where is it going?
(draw or write below)

Dad – answer

List 3 things you are proud of your son for this year:

_____

_____

_____

Optional: After you both have answered, discuss or write why you chose your answers or if you were surprised by each others choices:

_____

_____

_____

_____

_____

_____

_____

_____

_____

_____

Son – answer

List 3 things you are proud of yourself for this year:

_____

_____

_____

Optional: After you both have answered, discuss or write why you chose your answers or if you were surprised by each others choices:

_____

_____

_____

_____

_____

_____

_____

_____

_____

_____

Your son woke up this morning fluent in a new language. What do you hope it is?

_____

Why?

_____

_____

What would you want it to be for yourself?

_____

Why?

_____

_____

Hola! Bonjour! Ciao!
Namaste! Salaam!
Ni Hau! Ola! Bula!

You woke up this morning fluent in a new language. What do you hope it is?

_____

Why?

_____

_____

What would you want it to be for your dad?

_____

Why?

_____

_____

Dad – answer first

What are 2 things you think you have done right in raising your son?

_____

_____

_____

_____

What is something you wish you had done better or different in raising your son?

_____

_____

_____

_____

What is one thing you could still improve on?

_____

_____

_____

_____

Read what your dad has written.

Place check marks next to the ones you agree with.

Place X's next to the ones you don't agree with.

What is one thing you will do the same in raising your children?

_____

_____

_____

_____

What is one thing you will do different in raising your children?

_____

_____

_____

_____

In your ideal job/career what has been the most important for you? Rank 1-7:

_____ Great location

_____ Rewarding/love it

_____ Lots of travel

_____ High income

_____ Great co-workers

_____ Lots of time off

_____ Makes a difference

Optional: After you both have answered, discuss or write why you chose what you did or if you were surprised by each others choices:

_____

_____

_____

_____

_____

_____

In your ideal job/career what will be the most important for you? Rank 1-7:

_____ Great location

_____ Rewarding/love it

_____ Lots of travel

_____ High income

_____ Great co-workers

_____ Lots of time off

_____ Makes a difference

Optional: After you both have answered, discuss or write why you chose what you did or if you were surprised by each others choices:

_____

_____

_____

_____

_____

_____

You're planning a fun day for you and your son. Rank what you think his top three choices would be:

	Going Fishing
	Escape Room
	Laser Tag or Paintball
	Video Game Day
	Go Carts
	Amusement Park
	Pool/Beach
	Bounce/Trampaline House

You and your dad are spending the day together. Rank what your top three choices for activities would be:

	Going Fishing
	Escape Room
	Laser Tag or Paintball
	Video Game Day
	Go Carts
	Amusement Park
	Pool/Beach
	Bounce/Trampaline House

Do you believe in miracles? yes / no

Why or why not? (write or discuss)

_____

_____

_____

_____

Do you believe in aliens? yes / no

Why or why not? (write or discuss)

_____

_____

_____

_____

Do you believe in ghosts? yes / no

Why or why not? (write or discuss)

_____

_____

_____

_____

Do you believe in miracles? yes / no

Why or why not? (write or discuss)

_____

_____

_____

_____

Do you believe in aliens? yes / no

Why or why not? (write or discuss)

_____

_____

_____

_____

Do you believe in ghosts? yes / no

Why or why not? (write or discuss)

_____

_____

_____

_____

Predict what your son will think is better of the choices below?:

	City	Country	
	Quiet time	Party time	
	Marvel	D.C.	
	Vampire	Werewolf	
	Surprises	Planned events	
	Extra Credit	Curve	
	Running	Swimming	
	Winning $20	Finding $20	
	Free appetizer	Free dessert	
	Book smart	Street smart	
	Chocolate	Vanilla	
	Stay up late	Sleep in late	

Which of the choices below is better?

	City	Country	
	Quiet Time	Party Time	
	Marvel	D.C.	
	Vampire	Werewolf	
	Surprises	Planned events	
	Extra Credit	Curve	
	Running	Swimming	
	Winning $20	Finding $20	
	Free appetizer	Free dessert	
	Book smart	Street smart	
	Chocolate	Vanilla	
	Stay up late	Sleep in late	

Circle the 3 life goals that you wish most for your son:

Being healthy

Having a successful career

Caring for others

Making the world a better place

Finding a life partner

Being rich

Having children

Being happy

Having close friends

Being famous

Exploring/Traveling

Optional: After you both have answered, discuss or write why you chose what you did or if you were surprised by each others choices:

_____

_____

_____

Circle the 3 life goals that you wish most for yourself:

Being healthy

Having a successful career

Caring for others

Making the world a better place

Finding a life partner

Being rich

Having children

Being happy

Having close friends

Being famous

Exploring/Traveling

Optional: After you both have answered, discuss or write why you chose what you did or if you were surprised by each others choices:

_____

_____

_____

It's the ZOMBIE APOCALYPSE - The only survivors are you and your son!

What three of your son's traits/skills will help you both to survive?

_____

_____

_____

What weapon would he use?

_____

What weapon would you use?

_____

It's the ZOMBIE APOCALYPSE – The only survivors are you and your dad!

What two of your traits/skills will help you both to survive?

_____

_____

What skill would you wish you had?

_____

What weapon would you use?

_____

Who is.....

	Me	Son
sillier?		
happier?		
more likely to break a rule?		
more kind?		
more likely to invent something?		
more logical?		
more likely to talk their way out of a speeding ticket?		
more honest?		
more ambitious?		

Son – answer

Who is.....

	Me	Dad
sillier?		
happier?		
more likely to break a rule?		
more kind?		
more likely to invent something?		
more logical?		
more likely to talk their way out of a speeding ticket?		
more honest?		
more ambitious?		

Which 3 qualities do you think your son needs most from you?

Encouragement	
Clear and consistent rules	
A sense of humor	
Listening without giving advice	
Genuine interest in activities	
Direction and guidance	
Setting a good example	
Open communication	
Unconditional love	
Understanding and forgiveness	

Optional: After you both have answered, discuss or write why you chose what you did or if you were surprised by each others choices:

_____

_____

_____

_____

_____

Pick the top 2 qualities you need most from your dad:

Encouragement	
Clear and consistent rules	
A sense of humor	
Listening without giving advice	
Genuine interest in activities	
Direction and guidance	
Setting a good example	
Open communication	
Unconditional love	
Understanding and forgiveness	

Optional: After you both have answered, discuss or write why you chose what you did or if you were surprised by each others choices:

_____

_____

_____

_____

_____

Dad – answer second

In what two ways are you and your son the most alike?

_____

_____

In what two ways are you and your son the most different?

_____

_____

Optional: After you both have answered, discuss or write why you chose what you did or if you were surprised by each others answers:

_____

_____

_____

_____

_____

_____

Son – answer first

In what two ways are you and your dad the most alike?

_____

_____

In what two ways are you and your dad the most different?

_____

_____

Optional: After you both have answered, discuss or write why you chose what you did or if you were surprised by each others answers:

_____

_____

_____

_____

_____

_____

Dad – answer

Check 3 things you'd like to do more of with your son:

_____ work on cars or build things

_____ play games

_____ have conversations

_____ be active (sports/walks/bike rides...)

_____ go out to lunch or dinner

_____ watch TV/just hang out

_____ play video games

_____ do art/projects/music

_____ go to a live sporting event

Son – answer

Check 3 things you'd like to do more of with your dad:

_____ work on cars or build things

_____ play games

_____ have conversations

_____ be active (sports/walks/bike rides...)

_____ go out to lunch or dinner

_____ watch TV/just hang out

_____ play video games

_____ do art/projects/music

_____ go to a live sporting event

So...it turns out you get a super power on your 40th birthday. What do you hope it is?

_____ mind control

_____ invisibility

_____ super strength

_____ super speed

_____ fly

How will you use it?

_____

_____

_____

_____

After answering..were you surprised by each others choices? How?

_____

_____

_____

_____

Son – answer

So...it turns out you get a super power on your 20th birthday. What do you hope it is?

_____ mind control

_____ invisibility

_____ super strength

_____ super speed

_____ fly

How will you use it?

_____

_____

_____

_____

After answering..were you surprised by each others choices? How?

_____

_____

_____

_____

Do you believe in karma? yes / no

Why or why not? (write or discuss)

_____

_____

_____

_____

Do you believe in love at first sight? yes / no

Why or why not? (write or discuss)

_____

_____

_____

_____

Do you believe in guardian angels? yes / no

Why or why not? (write or discuss)

_____

_____

_____

_____

Do you believe in karma? yes / no

Why or why not? (write or discuss)

_____

_____

_____

_____

Do you believe in love at first sight? yes / no

Why or why not? (write or discuss)

_____

_____

_____

_____

Do you believe in guardian angels? yes / no

Why or why not? (write or discuss)

_____

_____

_____

_____

You just won a time travel trip!

Do you want to go:

_____   to the past

_____   to the future

what period of time in the past or how far into the future?

_____

_____

What would you want to see or do?

_____

_____

After answering..were you surprised by each others choices? How?

_____

_____

_____

_____

Son – answer

You just won a time travel trip!

Do you want to go:

_____ to the past

_____ to the future

what period of time in the past or how far into the future?

_____

_____

What would you want to see or do?

_____

_____

After answering..were you surprised by each others choices? How?

_____

_____

_____

_____

Do you think your son has ever...

	yes	no
Eaten a bug?		
Been in a physical fight?		
Been bullied?		
Had a crush?		
Lied about his age?		
Stayed up all night?		
Seen something illegal?		
Sent an email or text by mistake?		
Gone skinny dipping?		
Hid something from you?		
Gotten away with something at school?		
Made a prank phone call?		
Been offered weed?		

When you're both done, check the ones on his side that are correct about you. Only do this if you can both handle the truth!

Do you think your dad has ever...

	yes	no
Eaten a bug?		
Been in a physical fight?		
Been bullied?		
Had a crush?		
Lied about his age?		
Stayed up all night?		
Seen something illegal?		
Sent an email or text by mistake?		
Gone skinny dipping?		
Hid something from you?		
Gotten away with something at school?		
Made a prank phone call?		
Been offered weed?		

When you're both done, check the ones on his side that are correct about you. Only do this if you can both handle the truth!

Your son just won a **Vacation Home** that he can use every weekend. The perfect place would be...(check one in each group)

located

_____   on the oceanfront

_____   in the mountains

_____   by a lake

with a great view of the

_____   sunrise

_____   sunset

There would be plenty of

_____   outdoor activities

_____   indoor activities

and lots of

_____   quiet time

_____   parties

Son – answer second

You just won a **Vacation Home** that you can use every weekend. The perfect place would be...(check one in each group)

located

_____ on the oceanfront

_____ in the mountains

_____ by a lake

with a great view of the

_____ sunrise

_____ sunset

There would be plenty of

_____ outdoor activities

_____ indoor activities

and lots of

_____ quiet time

_____ parties

Rank these places in the order that you would like to stay in for a month (1=1st choice)...

Rank these places in the order that you would like to stay in for a month (1=1st choice)...

Dad – draw your son's favorite

fast food

sport to play

dessert

animal

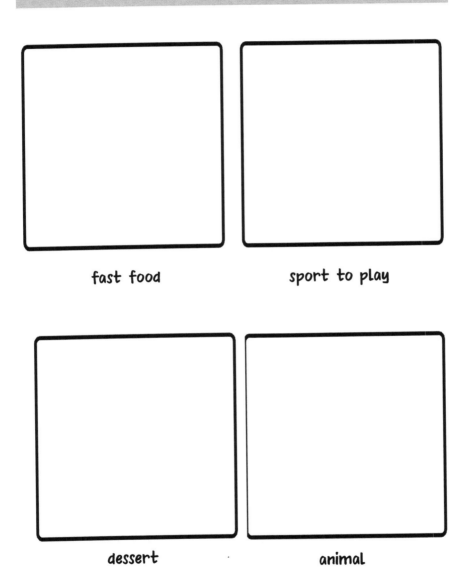

fast food

sport to play

dessert

animal

Check 3 things you hope your son knows:

_____ how much I love him

_____ what a great person I think he is

_____ how much I worry about him

_____ how much I believe in him

_____ how much I trust him

_____ how special he is

_____ how much I expect of him

Son – answer

Check 3 things you hope your dad knows:

_____ that I'm trying

_____ that there are a lot of pressures on me

_____ that I'm not an idiot

_____ that he can trust me

_____ that I'm not going to do anything really stupid

_____ that I need space to grow

_____ that I think about my future

Dad – answer

Question:

_____

_____

_____

Answer:

_____

_____

_____

_____

_____

_____

_____

_____

_____

_____

_____

_____

_____

_____

_____

_____

Son – answer

Question:

_____

_____

_____

Answer:

_____

_____

_____

_____

_____

_____

_____

_____

_____

_____

_____

_____

_____

_____

_____

Dad – answer

Question:

_____

_____

_____

Answer:

_____

_____

_____

_____

_____

_____

_____

_____

_____

_____

_____

_____

_____

_____

_____

_____

_____

_____

_____

Son – answer

Question:

_____

_____

_____

Answer:

_____

_____

_____

_____

_____

_____

_____

_____

_____

_____

_____

_____

_____

_____

_____

_____

Dad – answer

Question:

_____

_____

_____

Answer:

_____

_____

_____

_____

_____

_____

_____

_____

_____

_____

_____

_____

_____

_____

_____

_____

Son – answer

Question:

_____

_____

_____

Answer:

_____

_____

_____

_____

_____

_____

_____

_____

_____

_____

_____

_____

_____

_____

_____

_____

Dad – answer

Question:

_____

_____

_____

Answer:

_____

_____

_____

_____

_____

_____

_____

_____

_____

_____

_____

_____

_____

_____

_____

_____

_____

Son – answer

Question:

_____

_____

_____

Answer:

_____

_____

_____

_____

_____

_____

_____

_____

_____

_____

_____

_____

_____

_____

_____

_____

Dad – answer

Question:

_____

_____

_____

Answer:

_____

_____

_____

_____

_____

_____

_____

_____

_____

_____

_____

_____

_____

_____

_____

_____

_____

Son – answer

Question:

_____

_____

_____

Answer:

_____

_____

_____

_____

_____

_____

_____

_____

_____

_____

_____

_____

_____

_____

_____

_____

_____

Dad – answer

Question:

_____

_____

_____

Answer:

_____

_____

_____

_____

_____

_____

_____

_____

_____

_____

_____

_____

_____

_____

_____

_____

_____

Son – answer

Question:

_____

_____

_____

Answer:

_____

_____

_____

_____

_____

_____

_____

_____

_____

_____

_____

_____

_____

_____

_____

Made in the USA
Middletown, DE
18 November 2020